# Rails Around Birmingham
## in photographs by Ray Fincham

Ex-LMS "Crab" No.42707 stands at Bromford Bridge Station awaiting signal clearance before continuing tender first east towards Water Orton. The locomotive, built in 1926 by Sir Henry Fowler to a design by his predecessor, George Hughes, had not much more than a year to serve before being withdrawn in October 1964. The photograph was taken in the summer of 1963, a time when we spent much of our long school holiday on the deserted platforms. The station closed in 1965, and the platforms and the race-course it served have gone, a large housing estate now occupying the space once the preserve of galloping horses and the racing set.

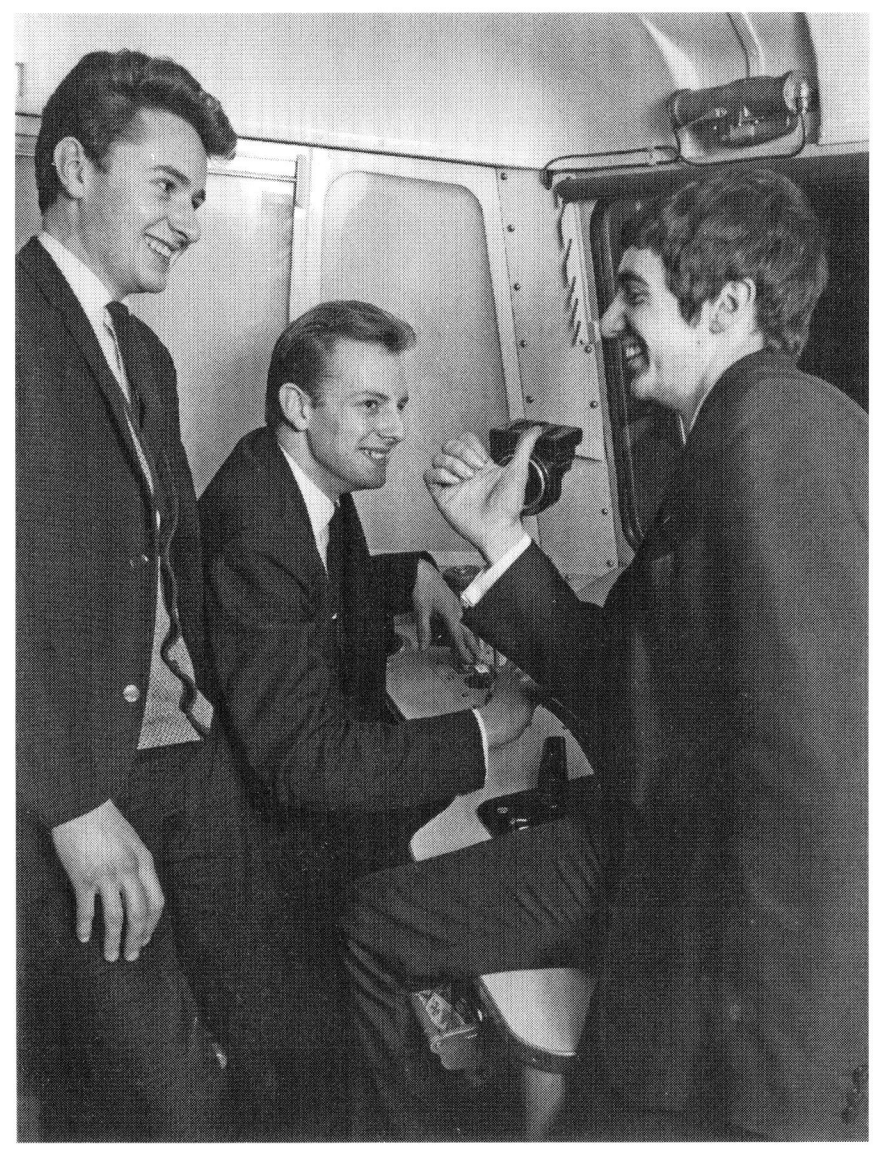

© Ray Fincham, 2018
First published in the United Kingdom, 2018,
by Stenlake Publishing Ltd.
54-58 Mill Square, Catrine, KA5 6RD
www.stenlake.co.uk
ISBN 978-1-84033-808-9

The publishers regret that they cannot supply copies of any pictures featured in this book.

Printed by
P2D Books, 1 Newlands Rd,
Westoning, Bedford, MK45 5LD

The author, right, pictured at the tender age of eighteen, posing for publicity shots aboard the driver training simulator which was based on the No.2-end cab of BR Type AL5 No. E3056. The occasion being marked was the conclusion of the 1966 CM&EE Apprentice of the Year competition in which he came third. The winner is at the controls.

# Introduction

The first half of the 1960s was a period of rapid change on Britain's railways, the headlong rush to replace steam locomotives with modern diesel and electric machines was evident to even the most casual observer. The root cause of the change was the announcement in 1955 of a plan to modernise the railway network.

Briefly going back to 1948 and the nationalisation of Britain's railways, one of the most pressing concerns then exercising the newly-formed Railway Executive was the state of the locomotive stock. The number of engines to hand then exceeded 20,300; they consisted of over 400 diverse types, and differed widely in their usefulness and state of repair. The result of their deliberations was seen in 1951, when freshly designed steam locomotives began to appear. These were the British Railways "Standard" types, a total of twelve designs being thought necessary to meet the different duties envisaged.

The design team, headed by Robert Riddles, expected their machines to have a lifespan of more than twenty years, by which time it was believed that all the major routes would be electrified; but by the time the last of the 999 Standard locomotives had been named Evening Star, the plan to phase out steam traction was already five years old.

Retuning now to 1955, orders were place for 174 diesel locomotives, ranging from 800bhp to 2400bhp. The understanding was that, before embarking on mass production, a period of three years would be necessary during which time the machines would be thoroughly evaluated. The need for such prudence was patently obvious, the manufactures having no experience of building such locomotives for the British market, and the end user having little experience of operating them.

Sadly, the trials were never completed, the decision being made to accelerate the replacement scheme occasioned by BR's dire financial situation; the expectation was that huge savings would result from the switch to diesel and electric traction. A further consideration was the rising cost of coal, some alarm also being caused when the National Coal Board warned that supplies could no longer be guaranteed.

By 1959, only 140 of the 174 locomotives ordered had been delivered; nevertheless, 900 more were placed on order. By 1961, well over a thousand main line diesels were in service, and almost as many were being procured. With nineteen different types plying their trade, any hope of standardisation had been lost.

Significant changes were occurring throughout the land; this book looks back to the period and depicts the hectic pace of such change as it had its effect on the railways around Birmingham. The period 1961 to 1966, portrayed by the photographs in the following pages was arguably that of most rapid change. Each month, without fail, steam engines were being withdrawn and disposed of, whilst shiny new diesels and electrics were taking their place. These were interesting times.

My own interest in railways began during the early part of this period, as my friends selflessly passed on their knowledge, making clear which numbers on a locomotive or multiple unit were significant and which were not.

I bought a copy of Ian Allan's "Combine" and was immediately hooked on the quest of gathering as many numbers as possible. Weekends were

Ex-Great Western Class "7400" 0-6-0 No.7413 waits with a down freight, the flat side of its pannier tank patterned by a combination of autumn sunlight and the decorative valance of Birmingham Snow Hill's platform awning, October 1963. A common sight throughout the Western Region, these numerous and versatile engines were to be seen on shunting, freight and local passenger duties.

spent trainspotting locally, or when funds permitted, wandering the country with organised enthusiast's clubs.

I also had a budding interest in photography, and unique among my peers, I began to take the family Box Brownie on some of my spotting trips.

Sometime during 1962 at the age of fourteen, I was given my first camera. This was very second-hand and old fashioned even by the standards of the early 1960s; it was a rather bulky fold-out bellows contraption with a tiny lens, although it produced a negative of respectable size using 120 film at 8 exposures to the roll.

I progressed to a more modern 35mm camera partway through 1964. This too was second-hand and had a small fixed lens and a direct vision viewfinder, but it was much more handy than my previous camera, and had the advantage of a faster shutter speed.

Standard Class "5MT" No.73068 catches the sun as it stands alongside ex-LMS "Black 5" No.44851 within the gloomy confines of Birmingham New Street station, May 1963. The BR Standard "5MT" introduced in 1951 was little more than a minor evolution of Stanier's highly successful "Black 5" design dating back to 1934. No.73068 would be withdrawn at the end of 1965, whilst its elder cousin soldiered on until April 1968, just four months short of the cessation of steam operation on British Railways' standard gauge network.

Soon I began to develop my own photographs, and having persuaded my parents to give up the space beneath the stairs, I was able to establish a tiny dark room. This pokey space I equipped with a homemade bench, a red light, and the requisite trays and chemicals.

A few early images were made by the simple contact print method and, though of relatively small size, the results were generally sharp and clear, but what I really wanted was an enlarger.

The quality of an enlarger depends chiefly on the quality of its optics. My budget would allow for the purchase of only the most basic instrument containing a very crude plastic lens. This explains the phenomenon which can clearly be seen in some early images where the centre of the photograph appears sharp and correctly focused, but towards the edges of the print, the image becomes somewhat blurred.

The better results were made using my school's enlarger, or were printed later, after I had managed to acquire a higher quality enlarger which featured a glass lens.

During 1964, I left school and began working for the railway's Chief Mechanical and Electrical Engineers Department as an apprentice electrician, a step which would lead to a life-time career in the railway industry. At this time I also met the girl who would later become my wife, and my enthusiasm for trainspotting began to wane.

The photographs in my collection have survived for over 50 years, although regrettably the negatives have been lost. For many years, the albums in which prints are contained were kept in a cardboard box, taken from house to house as we moved around, stored in various lofts, garages and sheds. From time to time, they would be borrowed by my younger brother John, who was by my side or occasionally in shot when I took many of the photographs.

Contained within this volume are photographs taken over those few years at the Western Region's Birmingham Snow Hill, and at the less well favoured Midland Region's New Street. Moving out of Birmingham, south along the L&NW line through the suburbs, shots as far as Marston Green are included. The Midland main line is also depicted out to Tamworth, where the electrified WCML also features. Many of the locations are now unrecognisable, half a century of history having taken effect. As for the locomotives, they, apart from a fortunate handful which survive in preservation, have each been cut-up and reduced to manageable fragments to feed the blast-furnaces, at a time when Britain still had a significant steel making industry.

# Birmingham Snow Hill

Snow Hill was a wonderful station, laid out in grand fashion. Four tracks separated the main platforms which were wide and spacious, and overall, the glazed roof kept us dry and provided a nice, though for a photographer, a sometimes troublesome diffused light. Ex-Great Western Class "4500" 2-6-2T No.4555 attracts a group of admirers as she waits with a five coach Stephenson Locomotive Society special to Bromyard, June 1964. The engine had been withdrawn from service during the previous year; purchased privately by Mr Patrick Whitehouse, restoration included a return to Great Western Railway livery. The concept of privately-owned locomotives was only just becoming established in the early 1960s. The pioneers involved in these early projects sparked a movement which expanded to encompass many hundreds of dedicated and hard-working enthusiasts, and eventually blossomed into today's preservation industry. The locomotive, now graced by the name *Warrior*, is at the time of writing undergoing a major overhaul in the workshops of the Paignton and Dartmouth Railway. A diesel multiple unit forming a local passenger service stands at platform 7.

Ex-Great Western "Hall" class No.6970 *Waddon Hall* waits at platform 12 with a south bound parcels train, Birmingham Snow Hill, November 1963. Parcel and luggage offices were accommodated in the cavernous space below the station. The station I knew and loved in the 1960s was not the first building on the site. The original station, opened in 1852 and named Livery Street, was little more than a simple wooden shed. It was renamed Snow Hill in 1858, and the prestigious Great Western Hotel was added in 1863. A few years later, the platforms were extended to accommodate longer trains, and the wooden structure, now almost twenty years old, was replaced by a more appropriate arched roof of iron and glass. The spacious station which is depicted in these pages was built during the period 1906 to 1912, and provided the needs of travellers for the next 60 years.

Ex-Great Western Class "8100" 2-6-2T No.8109 stands at the south end of Snow Hill Station, October 1963. The locomotive pictured was the final example of ten such engines rebuilt from Churchward Class "5101s", and emerged from Swindon Works in November 1939. Fittingly, it was also the last of the class to be withdrawn, this latter event occurring in June 1965. The stairway seen above the locomotive gave access to the down platforms from the main booking hall which was off Colmore Row. Entry to the station was obtained only after purchase of a platform ticket, a necessary part of the day's expenditure.

*Right:* Ex-Great Western "Castle" Class 4-6-0 No.7026 *Powis Castle* stands at platform 5 at the head of a north bound Saturday excursion train, August 1963. Built by C.B.Collett for express passenger duties, the first of the class was out-shopped from Swindon in 1923. Production continued through to 1950, by which time 155 examples had been built together with a further sixteen, which had been converted from other classes. The engines performed superbly and handled all but the heaviest passenger trains. *Powis Castle* was built in 1949 and fitted with a double chimney ten years later. The modification, in conjunction with the addition of larger superheaters, further improved the locomotive's ability to sustain high speed running.

*Left:* The hasty introduction of diesel types, and the lack of time to evaluate the differing designs, led inevitably to some loss of investment as locomotives failed to meet expectations. Perhaps the most notorious waste however, resulted from the decision to allow the Western Region to go its own way, and purchase diesel-hydraulic locomotives. The argument in favour of the transmission arrangement is that of comparatively good power to weight ratio, although this is offset by a complexity of design and more onerous maintenance requirements. A total of six classes of diesel-hydraulic machines were produced between 1958 and 1964, most working reasonably well, but the increasing cost of maintenance and a perceived lack of reliability resulted inevitably in a premature end to this experiment. One of the more successful of the diesel-hydraulic types was the 2700bhp British Railways "Western" Class. Pictured here in May 1963, No. D1000 *Western Enterprise*, in experimental "Desert Sand" livery, waits to continue its journey northwards. Although responsible for ousting the much loved "Kings" from their place on express passenger workings, many enthusiasts had a high regard for this stylish class.

Ex-Great Western "5600" Class 0-6-2T No.6667 comes to a stand with a down mineral train, Birmingham Snow Hill, June 1963. The tank engines were constructed to a design by C.B. Collett for passenger and goods services in the Welsh Valleys. One hundred and fifty of these versatile locomotives were built at Swindon, but a batch of 50, including this example, were built during 1938 by Armstrong Whitworth at their Newcastle-on-Tyne works. No.6667 was withdrawn from service towards the end of 1965 and cut up at Long Marston the following year. No fewer than nine of the class survive in various states of preservation.

All appears effortless as British Railways Standard Class "9F" No.92234 completes the 1:47 climb up from Hockley, soon to pass through Snow Hill Station on the up centre road with a south bound freight. Some 251 of these powerful locomotives were built between 1954 and 1960, but the swift onset of dieselisation condemned them to a brief working life. One intriguing feature of the locomotive design concerns the centre pair of driving wheels, which lacked flanges, thus enabling the massive 2-10-0 locomotive to negotiate curves as tight as 400ft in radius; a situation not encountered at Birmingham Snow Hill.

Ex-Great Western "County" Class 4-6-0 No.1000 *County of Middlesex* makes ready to restart from the north end of Birmingham Snow Hill, June 1964. Produced in Swindon between 1945 and 1947, these Hawksworth-designed locomotives had a relatively short working life, the whole class being withdrawn by the end of 1964. Lamentably, all 30 examples were scrapped, but an ambitious scheme currently underway will see a replica of 1014 *County of Glamorgan* taking shape over the next few years. The project, being undertaken by the Great Western Society, will utilise the frames of a "Modified Hall" and the boiler from a Stanier "8F" in a reconstruction of the locomotive type.

Snow Hill's through lines were always busy with freight trains, for the most part steam hauled, by anything from a lowly 0-6-0 tank to a powerful Standard class 2-10-0. Here, ex-Great Western Class "5101" 2-6-2T No.4111 comes to a halt between the Great Charles Street bridge girders, Birmingham Snow Hill, August 1963. A total of 140 of the class were built, this machine being turned out of Swindon Works in 1936.

The driver of BR Standard "9F" No.92085 looks out for the signal to clear before proceeding tender first under the city centre, Birmingham Snow Hill, October 1963. The powerful 2-10-0 would be withdrawn at the end of 1966 having spent just ten years in service. After its withdrawal, the locomotive was taken to Woodhams' scrapyard at Barry Island near Cardiff. Many of the engines which entered Dai Woodhams' scrapyard were fortunate enough to be rescued by individuals and preservation societies, but No.92085 was not among their number, the "9F" being reduced to 86 tons of scrap during 1980.

Ex-Great Western "Modified Hall" No.7908 *Henshall Hall* waits in the carriage sidings at the north end of Birmingham Snow Hill with rolling stock to form a local passenger service, May 1964. Although clearly in need of a clean, the locomotive appears to be in good condition, with name and number plates still in place. The nameplates in particular, formed of brass letters mounted on gracefully arched blanks, typify GWR individuality and style, and reveal in part, the charm which has bewitched and captivated so many enthusiasts over the years.

Ex-Great Western "Grange," No.6853 *Morehampton Grange*, comes to rest with an up freight in November 1963. During the following year the locomotive was subject to a heavy overhaul at Swindon Works, emerging in tip-top condition during August. Sadly, by October the engine was withdrawn from service. It had long been the case that locomotives would end their days back at main works, but by the 1960s, with a plethora of steam engines waiting to be dismembered, private scrapyards throughout the country were contracted to meet the demand. *Morehampton Grange* was dispatched to one such company, Cohens of Kettering, where it was cut up. It now seems unforgivable that not a single example of this very able class of 80 locomotives escaped scrapping.

The "9Fs" were very much part of the 1960s scene, although they disappeared far too rapidly. Here, No.92245 is pictured as it trundles through Birmingham Snow Hill with a down freight in June 1964. The locomotive, built at Crewe in 1958, was withdrawn just six years later, and is another of the many redundant steam engines to be dispatched to Woodhams' scrapyard at Barry Island, arriving there in May 1965. A handful of locomotives which I photographed during this period are still with us, including this engine. Some 60 years have elapsed since No.92245 was rolled out of the works, but now it seems that the "9F" is on the very edge of survival.

Towards the end of the 1980s, the land occupied by Woodhams' passed into council ownership, along with the ten locomotives which still rested there, No.92245 being one such machine. Seen here in September 2008 safely under cover within the former EWS depot at Barry Island, the locomotive endured a quarter of a century out in the open, a period during which cannibalisation and the elements had taken their toll. It now seems that the engine will be dismantled and sectioned to form an exhibit, part of a display planned for Barry to illustrate the history of Woodhams' scrapyard. The exhibition will explain how it came to pass that 213 of the 297 locomotives which entered the yard were saved, thus forming the nucleus of today's stock of preserved steam engines.

Ex-Great Western "Hall" Class 4-6-0 No.6915 *Mursley Hall* stands in the summer sunshine after arriving at Birmingham Snow Hill, 1964. A good many of the locomotives used for passenger duties were still well turned out at this time, and some care has been taken in the preparation of this engine, although it seems that the front number plate has been replaced with a well-made replica. It was a sad day when in 1972 Snow Hill Station was closed. The adjoining Great Western Hotel had been demolished in 1969, and by 1977, much of the station had followed it to the skip. The track between the two main platforms was torn up, and the space created used as a car park. British Railways was accused of corporate vandalism as the station lay rotting, a situation not uncommon throughout the country. One commentator even accused BR of causing the greatest act of architectural savagery since the Tudor dissolution of the monasteries. There was to be something of a reprieve for Snow Hill, and, fifteen years after it closed, trains once again graced its platforms; but this was not the Snow Hill of old, and the rebuild had reduced the station to a shadow of its former self.

# New Street and the L&NW Line South.

British Railways "Britannia" Class 4-6-2 No.70031 *Byron* at the head of a train of empty coaching stock, Birmingham New Street, June 1964. The platforms here are well below street level, and concurrent with the electrification of the line, a concrete raft was built over the site to provide space above for station facilities and a city centre shopping mall. So thoroughly were the platforms enclosed that today, Birmingham New Street is classified as an underground station.

Later the same day, having been turned, *Byron* exits Birmingham New Street with a north bound passenger service. The station was undergoing a major re-build at this time, and the structure above the locomotive is a temporary bridge, a tiny element in the complex staging works required to keep the station functioning during the £2.5 million rebuilding process completed by 1967.

Introduced hastily in 1934, Stanier's 4-6-0 "Jubilee" class suffered design faults which resulted in poor steaming, and several changes were required before the problem was rectified. Once modified, the locomotives proved themselves to be popular workhorses, and members of the class were often to be seen in charge of the faster cross-country passenger services. Such a duty sees 45552 *Silver Jubilee* re-starting its south bound train from Birmingham New Street in early 1964. The locomotive had been named in 1935 to honour the twenty fifth year of the reign of King George V, and served first the LMS then British Railways until its withdrawal in September 1964.

D230 *Scythia* and sister engine D369 arrive at Birmingham New Street with a train from Euston, early 1964. Double heading of express passenger services on the route was far from common in the era of English Electric Type 4s, a single 2000bhp locomotive being capable of handling the duty. The doors fitted to cab ends to provide gangway connection between units when coupled together were rarely used and were subsequently removed.

Introduced in 1951, British Railways Standard Class "7P6F" became better known as "Britannia" Pacifics after the first named of the class. Made ready for its next turn of duty, No.70000 *Britannia* moves off Crewe North shed, June 1964. Although photographed at Crewe, there exists a tenuous connection with the Midlands. Note the distortion to the frame in the region of the front buffer beam, damage sustained in a collision at Birmingham New Street. The locomotive was withdrawn from service two years after this shot was taken, and is one of only two of the class to have been preserved

Ex-LMS Ivatt Class "2MT" No.46427 on shunting duties, Stechford, December 1963. A total of 128 such locomotives were built between 1946 and 1952, and no fewer than seven examples have been saved in preservation. The scene at Stechford has changed radically since this photograph was taken, and the goods yard pictured has been removed. The site, east of the station, is now occupied by Stechford Trading Estate.

Our favoured spot when out on the ex-London and North Western line south of Birmingham was at a boarded crossing partway between Lea Hall and Marston Green. Here, in the summer of 1964, ex-LMS "Black 5" No.44870 is seen in charge of a down semi-fast passenger train. Steam haulage of passenger services was very much in decline at this time, a Type 2 or English Electric Type 4 diesel more normally being seen. The little-used boarded crossing has, in these days of heightened health and safety concerns, been replaced by a little-used footbridge.

Trips to Lea Hall would sometimes be undertaken during the long summer evenings to see "The Cement". A small group of us would cycle the few miles to the track side; our friend Malcolm had no bike, but he was a runner. We would cycle along at reduced pace with Malcolm reassuring us that jogging to keep up with us was the most natural thing in the world. "The Cement" was a regular freight train working, which we understood to start at Rugby, and would contain a group of cement wagons carrying the product of that town northwards. Sometimes, we would be disappointed, and the train would fail to make its appearance. At other times, it would run, but be hauled by a "Black 5" or a diesel. The big reward however, was when the train was headed by a "Britannia" Class locomotive, and despite the mundane nature of the task, a "Brit" was allocated to the duty on a regular basis. This would make up for any previous disappointments, "A Brit on the Cement" making the journey home a joyous occasion, and Malcolm would bounce along like a true athlete. British Railways "Britannia" Class Pacific No.70020 *Mercury* approaching Lea Hall with a down freight train in the summer of 1964.

Returning home with their Christmas shopping, passengers alight from the Birmingham to Northampton train at Marston Green, December 1963. The six car service, with Metropolitan-Cammell twin unit Driving Trailer No.M56334 leading, is completed by two Gloucester R.C.& W. Co. twin units. Once reviled, nostalgia now abounds for such conveyances, and many preserved railways depend on them when not running steam-hauled services. A modern booking hall now occupies the site of the erstwhile signal box.

British Railways Derby-built Type 2 diesel-electric No. D5013 passes through Marston Green with a Birmingham bound service, December 1963. The steel masts, much in evidence, each placed within its cast concrete foundation would soon support the overhead line equipment. The electrification scheme was completed ready for a full electric timetable in April 1966, by which time diesel power would be relegated to a minor role. The platforms at Marston Green have been extended since this photograph was taken, and the level crossing is no more. The platform extension on the up side of the track occupies the site of the coal merchants huts, and the old goods yard beyond is now a station car park, with housing occupying the eastern end of the site. Incidentally, my brother John, swathed in duffle coat, can be seen making haste to the track side. Our pushbikes lean unlocked against the railings.

# The Midland Main Line & Tamworth.

Ex-WD "Austerity" 2-8-0 No.90038 clanks through Bromford Bridge with a Birmingham bound coal train, September 1963. Built for the War Department to a simple design, construction of the class commenced in January 1943. So rapid was the building process that by the end of hostilities in Europe in May 1945, the number of "Austerity" locomotives shipped overseas totalled one thousand. Remarkably 733 of the 2-8-0s saw service with British Railways.

Ex-LMS "Jubilee" Class 4-6-0 No.45620 *North Borneo* was out-shopped from Crewe Works in 1934, and after a working life of 30 years was withdrawn from service in September 1964. Pictured here at Bromford Bridge just a few months prior to that sad day, *North Borneo* was put to the torch in January of the following year.

British Railways Standard Class "9F" No.92248 passes Bromford Bridge Station at the start of its journey south to Fawley with a train of empty Esso tank wagons, January 1964. On the journey north from Fawley's oil refinery, the fully-laden wagons would be carrying 100,000 gallons of petrol to Bromford. Hauling such a train, weighing in at 1,200 tons, was an onerous task, nevertheless a solitary "9F" was capable of fulfilling the duty. The station at Bromford Bridge was built in 1856 to serve the nearby racetrack, and had no regular passenger service, the platforms used only by "Race Day Specials" when meetings were being held.

Ex-LMS "8F" No.48637 with an up goods train, seen here at Bromford Bridge Station in the summer of 1964. The "8F" was one Stanier's many successes, locomotives to this design being produced at various works throughout the land. No.48637 was a product of Brighton, and was one of 93 built there at a rapid pace during 1943 and 1944 for the War Department at a time when such motive power was desperately needed, both at home and overseas. At the end of hostilities, and following nationalisation in 1948, ownership passed to British Railways. In a lighter vain, note the inspector's attire. Several years would pass before those whose job took them out on the track would be obliged to wear high-visibility clothing.

Castle Bromwich was our nearest station, and here, on the 1st January 1964, ex-LMS Class "8F" No.48380 is seen with an east bound freight emerging from beneath Chester Road on the station avoiding line. Note the gas lighting on the platform, a means of illumination quite common on smaller stations at this time. Much change has occurred since this date, the station, opened in 1842 and rebuilt by the Midland Railway in 1901 was once busy, used daily by hundreds of local factory workers; but in 1968 the station closed, former passengers had been made redundant as the manufacturers hereabouts closed their gates, or for those who had retained their jobs, the commute would generally be done by car. The structures pictured have since been swept away by the widening of the road bridge.

Water Orton was one of our favourite venues, a cycle ride from home into what we Brummies considered to be countryside. Our enthusiasm, however, would have been tested on this cold and frosty day in December 1963. Class "9F" No.92027, one of the few to be fitted with a Crosti boiler, makes a spirited getaway as it crosses over to the Nuneaton bound line with a heavy freight train. Just ten of the 251 "9Fs" were built with the Italian-designed Crosti boiler in an endeavour to improve efficiency. The hoped-for reduction in coal consumption was never realised, and the boilers were converted to a more orthodox arrangement, although the locomotives retained their distinctive smoke boxes throughout their short service lives. All ten examples were withdrawn by the end of 1967 and subsequently cut up.

How natural it must have seemed when faced with a long list of diesels, to assign to the first locomotive the number D1, but what a stroke of genius it was to name it in such noble a fashion, after England's highest mountain. Odd though, that the name of the higher Welsh peak was carried by sister engine D9, and that Scotland's Ben Nevis was left unrecognised. British Railways Type 4 "Peak" Class diesel-electric No. D1 *Scafell Pike* with coal for Birmingham, passing Water Orton in the spring of 1964. Often looking grimy and unkempt, it had long been common to see the "namers" D1 to D10 hauling coal around the Midlands. Their output was 200bhp less than the 2500bhp rating of others in the class which were regularly used on passenger services.

A view from the footbridge taken in the summer of 1963 sees Class "4F" 0-6-0 No.44571 proceeding rapidly through Water Orton towards Birmingham. These diminutive engines seemed capable, when running light, of speeds out of all proportion to their size, particularly when making their way home to Saltley. Designed by Sir Henry Fowler for the London Midland & Scottish Railway Company and introduced in 1924, a total of four of the class have been preserved. The lines to the left are those for Derby and the north east; Nuneaton lines run to the right.

Here in the summer of 1966, Brush Type 4 No. D1963 ambles through Water Orton East Junction from the Nuneaton line with a train-load of steel bars. Between 1962 and 1967, 528 of these locomotives were built at Crewe and the Brush Works at Loughborough. So numerous did the type become that they represented almost half the BR diesel fleet rated at 2000bhp and above. The locomotive pictured, built at Crewe and introduced in September 1965, gave over 40 years of service before being scrapped in November 2007.

Diesel Multiple Units would generally provide local Birmingham to Derby services at this time. Here in the spring of 1964, BR Standard "4MT" No.76086, with a three coach train, is seen shortly after departure from Water Orton, and is likely to have been a last minute substitution for a failed "bog unit". I always assumed that the interest I received from train crew was a form of approbation. I realised much later that their intense looks were more likely to have been ones of condemnation for trespass upon the railway.

Dramatic close-up shots at Water Orton necessitated a jump down from a high retaining wall, getting back up was more difficult. Here, in the summer of 1966, British Railways "Peak" Class diesel-electric No. D130, in fine condition, trundles by East Junction signal box with a fully fitted goods train bound for the north east. It's probable that the signal box, later to be re-used as a permanent way office, was out of use at this date. The structure has since been removed.

Prior to its disposal at Derby Works, ex-Midland Railway Class "2F-1" No.58186 was stored for a while in a Water Orton siding subsequent to its withdrawal in January 1961. The Johnson-designed 0-6-0 locomotive had a remarkably long working life; having been built at Derby in 1876, it served first the Midland Railway, then the LMS and finally British Railways for a grand total of 85 years before being retired.

British Railways "Peak" No. D131 negotiates the east junction at Water Orton in the summer of 1964. A total of 193 of these dependable machines were built at Derby and Crewe in three distinct batches between 1959 and 1963. When Total Operating Processing Scheme (TOPS) numbering was extended to locomotives in 1971, the "Peaks" were recognised as classes 44, 45 and 46 to reflect those differences. Under the new numbering system, D131 became No. 45.074. The train is on the down main line from Derby and the north east and will travel on via Birmingham and Bristol to its destination in the south west.

BR&WC Type 2 No. D5386 makes its way across Water Orton East Junction onto the Nuneaton bound lines with an up freight working in the summer of 1966. Built not so very far away at the Birmingham Railway Carriage and Wagon Works at Smethwick, the locomotive was one of the final batch of 37 of the class which were allocated to the Midland Region. By the end of the decade, the whole of the class had been moved to the Scottish Region, and in 1973, the locomotive was renumbered 27.103. The fitting of electric train heating in the mid 1970s, and the adaptation to push-pull working saw another number change, and as 27.212, it was used on the Edinburgh to Glasgow service. The majority of diesel locomotives which I photographed during the 1960s have now been dismantled and disposed of, but D5386 remains extant.

By 1983, no longer required on push-pull duties, a final renumbering took place, and the engine served out its days in Scotland bearing the number 27.066. The whole of the Class 27 fleet was withdrawn by July 1987, but 27.066 was saved from the scrap-heap, and in 1988, taken to the North Norfolk Railway where it was restored to original condition, and numbered again D5386. After serving there for some fifteen years, the locomotive was purchased by the Dean Forest Railway. Pictured here at Norchard, the locomotive, painted in Rail Blue livery and carrying the number 27.066, performed regular duties on the line between Lydney Junction and Parkend. More recently, the locomotive has found a home at Barrow Hill.

Ex-LMS Stanier "Black 5" No.45232 approaching Water Orton with a down freight train in June 1964. The "Black 5s" were remarkably reliable engines, and averaged in excess of 150,000 miles between general repairs, they were still to be found working in the north west up to the last day of steam, 11th August 1968. Note the freshly painted smoke box suggesting that the locomotive had been into main works for a partial overhaul, a not uncommon sight towards the end of the steam era.

Tamworth was a station which was off-limits to trainspotters, and my collection contains few photographs taken from the platforms. Here, on New Year's Day 1964, I managed to capture the sight of British Railways Class "9F" No.92221 with a south bound freight just as our train pulled into the High Level platform. The station was re-built in conjunction with the West Coast Main Line modernisation scheme, and has altered little in the years since this snatched shot was taken.

A boarded crossing a mile or so north of Tamworth Station was our favoured location when trainspotting on the West Coast Main Line, and here, British Railways Type AL5 No. E3079 is seen heading north with a train of empty car-flats in the summer of 1966. During the late 1950s and early 60s small batches of locomotives for use on 25kV. electrified lines were ordered from a variety of manufacturers. This locomotive was one of a batch of twenty introduced in 1962 and built by British Railways at Doncaster Works with equipment supplied by British Thomson-Houston.

Type AL6 locomotives were steadily introduced during 1965 and 1966, ready for completion of the Euston to Manchester and Liverpool electrification scheme. The successful design of this class of which 100 were produced, stemmed from the experience gained whilst operating and maintaining the preceding types. No. E3163 waits for parcels to be loaded before continuing south, Tamworth Low Level, summer 1966. The dramatic shadow is provided by the over-bridge which carries the Birmingham-Derby lines across the Trent Valley section of the West Coast Main Line at this point. Passengers for Derby gain access to their trains by ascending the stairway signposted to the right of the photograph.

Type AL6 No. E3192 heads north with a fully-loaded car carrying train along with the additional burden of an unidentified Type AL5, Tamworth, summer 1966. One flaw in the AL6 design, which soon became apparent, was its adverse effect on the track, its nose suspended traction motors transmitting excessive stress to the permanent way. The problem was overcome by fitting additional helical spring suspension to support the weight of the locomotive body. The majority of the class, including E3192, were modified and thus allowed to continue to work at 100mph, whilst the unmodified locomotives were limited to 80mph freight only duties. By the mid 1980s however, with the need for more high-speed locomotives, the rest of the class were modified. The locomotive pictured was renumbered 86.247 under the TOPS system, and, on the 19th March 1981, was endowed with the name *Abraham Darby*, in honour of the 16th century iron-founder and pioneer industrialist.

British Railways Type AL5 No. E3061 with a down passenger train to the north of Tamworth, July 1964. The locomotive was built at Doncaster in 1961, and was one of fourteen of the class to be converted to freight only use in the 1980s. Renumbered 85.101, the locomotive continued to serve on the West Coast route until its withdrawal at the end of 1991. Following its retirement, the locomotive was stored at Crewe prior to being purchased by Pete Waterman in 1992, but was subsequently sold to the AC Locomotive Group in 1997.

Moved then to Barrow Hill, restoration began in 2000, and in 2002, No. 85.101 was painted in Railfreight Distribution livery, a paint scheme never applied during its service with British Railways. The following year, the locomotive was displayed at Doncaster for the works open day, and named *Doncaster Plant 150, 1853-2003*, in recognition of one and a half centuries of activity at Doncaster Works. A major electrical restoration is planned, and it is hoped that a return to working order is feasible. Pictured here on Barrow Hill in August 2008, No. 85.101 is the sole remaining example of this successful class.

A rake of newly introduced Mk.2 coaches form the Liverpool to London express seen speeding towards Tamworth behind British Railways Doncaster-built Type AL6 No. E3120, summer 1966. The route here has recently been upgraded from two to four tracks, and this naturally required a similar change to the over-head line equipment. Each mast or structure supporting the OHL is assigned a unique identifying number, and that to the left of the photograph is labelled "G" for the route, the next number telling us that we are in the 110th mile from Euston whilst the final number indicates that this is the 67th structure within that mile. Each of the masts pictured have now been removed, and portal structures spanning all four tracks have been installed to support the wires.

# Midlands Sheds

The small four-road brick-built shed at Leamington Spa was a Great Western depot by origin, but was transferred to Midland Region ownership in January 1963. On this murky day in December 1963, examples of LMS and GWR-designed 2-6-2 tank engines can be seen resting side by side. No. 41272 is the Ivatt designed ex-LMS offering; Class "5101" No.4151 represents the best traditions of Great Western design. The diesel shunter is No. D3974. The shed was closed on 14th June 1965, and is today the site of an industrial estate.

One hundred and twenty Class "2251" 0-6-0 tender locomotives were built at Swindon to a design by Charles Collett for medium powered goods duties. No.3271 was produced in 1947, just prior to nationalisation. Seen here at Leamington Spa shed in December 1963, the locomotive would spend a further twelve months in service before being withdrawn at the end of 1964. Just a single example of the class has survived.

Tyseley shed was opened in July 1908 as a two turntable structure together with a repair shop which became known as "The Factory". The facilities remained largely unchanged until 1963, when one of the two roundhouses was demolished to make way for a DMU depot, and by the following year, "The Factory" was razed to the ground to enable a diesel repair depot to be built. Pictured outside Tyseley's then new Diesel Multiple Unit Depot, on a cold December day in 1963, stands one of the Western Region's eight car Blue Pullman trains, motor brake second No.W60096 leading. These luxurious air-conditioned sets were introduced in 1960, and were used to provide the premiere Wolverhampton via Birmingham Snow Hill to London Paddington service. The long exposure time made necessary by the dull conditions is nicely demonstrated by the movement of the rather furtive looking trainspotters to the right of shot.

British Railways "Western" Class. diesel-hydraulic No. D1015 *Western Champion* was built at Swindon, entering service in January 1963, and was still painted in its experimental "Golden Ochre" livery when photographed on the wheel lathe at Tyseley in the December of the same year. Enjoying a working life of just thirteen years, *Western Champion* was withdrawn from service in December 1976 after sustaining damage in a derailment, having covered a grand total of 1,296,000 miles. A victim to the policy of standardisation on the more reliable diesel-electric types, all 74 of the "Western" Class locomotives were withdrawn by 1978. The popularity of these engines amongst enthusiasts did, however, ensure that seven of the locomotives, including *Western Champion*, survive in preservation.

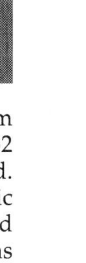

Class 52 diesel-hydraulic No. D1015 *Western Champion*, looking resplendent in maroon livery, arrives at Liverpool Lime Street with a special train from Salisbury, 21st July 2008. The trip was organised to coincide with Liverpool's Tall Ships Festival and this was claimed to be the first time that a Class 52 had visited the city. The locomotive, withdrawn in December 1976, spent more than three years in store at Swindon before work to cut her up commenced. Fortunately, at the 11th hour, *Western Champion* was purchased by the Diesel Traction Group for £6,125, and restored at Swindon, its first public appearance being at an Old Oak Common open day in September 1985. Some years later, *Western Champion* benefited from a major rebuild, which allowed mainline running, the necessary certificate being granted in January 2002. Since then, the locomotive has earned its keep hauling enthusiast's specials as well as making regular appearances at various rail galas.

Saltley shed was a substantial structure containing three turntables. We would often enter this shed on an unofficial basis, but I stopped taking my camera along after one occasion when we were chased from the gloom of the roundhouse by a uniformed bobby, only making good our escape after scampering out across the yard and jumping down to the canal tow path. Pictured here in December 1963, ex-Midland "4F" 0-6-0 No.44180 can be seen in the gloom, with ex-LMS "Crab" No.42763 to the left. The building was subsequently stripped of its roof, but Saltley continued to house steam engines until they were displaced wholly by diesels in early 1967.

Aston was a large shed, its twelve roads capable of housing up to 60 locomotives, but photography was difficult within its tightly packed confines. The yard there was comparatively small, and the best subject to be found on this December day in 1963 was that of the ubiquitous diesel shunter. Nine hundred and ninety six of these 400bhp machines were built between 1953 and 1966, by which time they had become the most numerous class of locomotives built for British Railways. No. D3020 was manufactured at Derby Works in 1953 and was in service for just twenty years, being withdrawn in 1973. Many shunting engines are still to be seen on Britain's railways today, and some 65 are in use on heritage railways. The other locomotive in the photo is also a product of Derby; British Railways Type 2 No. D5017 emerged from the works in June 1959. Aston Motive Power Depot was closed on 11th October 1965. The site is occupied now by more modern sheds, serving the needs of commercial buses and trucks.

With the paraphernalia of re-coaling well in evidence, Stanier Class "8F" 2-8-0 No.48101 moves slowly about Bescot yard in early 1964. The locomotive was one of a batch of 137 built at Crewe between 1935 and 1944 for heavy freight work, and emerged from the works in 1938. The depot was closed to steam in 1966, although the engine shed was retained for wagon repairs. A purpose built diesel depot was established in 1989.